MAINTAIN
A
COOL AND CALM
HARMONY....

Birister Sharma

Copyright © 2022 Birister Sharma

All Rights Reserved.

Dedicated to my loving wife….

Pallabi Devi Sharma

I surrendered to you, O my Lord……

"Om Namah Shivaya"

Table of Contents

One word

Anything can happen in your life. You never know what will happen next.

Life is always full of ups and downs. You've got to accept every up and down in your life. You've got to accept your successes and failures.

Not everything is important. You've got to focus only on the important things in your life. Don't divert your mind, heart, and soul to unimportant things.

Nobody is perfect in this world. If you're not perfect, then don't worry. Believe in yourself. Just work with your own potential and lead yourself to excellence.

Never underestimate anybody. Never underestimate your own potential and talents, either. Dig out your own hidden treasure inside you.

Solve your own problem. Nobody will solve your problem. Never depend on anybody to solve your problem. Only you can solve your own problem.

Nobody knows you better than you know yourself. You're the best person to understand yourself. You know what is good for you and what is bad for you.

Never blame anybody, but accept your mistakes. Try to amend your mistakes the very moment you recognize them. Don't wait for anybody to correct your mistakes; correct your own mistakes straightaway.

Be flexible in your life. Don't be too tough and harsh on yourself. Love yourself and maintain your own balance in life.

You are not always right. Before you execute anything in your life, think before you act, and consider the viewpoints of other people. Don't jump to conclusions too early. Take your time.

Whatever you do in your life, wherever you live your life, whatever the situation—whether good or bad, whether you're successful or a failure in your life, whether you're fighting or struggling—never lose your mental state of cool and calmness. Always keep your cool and calm in every situation in your life. This is the only way to lead your own life.

~***~

1. Anything can happen

Do you know what will happen now, today, and tomorrow in your life?

Can you predict anything?

Certainly not. Only Almighty God knows.

You can't predict anything. Everything is uncertain and a mystery in your life. Anything can happen in your life. But you should never give up anything in your life. You should never quit in your life. After all, this is called life.

Life is always uncertain and a mystery. Anything can happen in your life. And in the midst of this uncertainty and mystery, you have to live your life.

Why should you wear a helmet when you ride a bike?

You should wear a helmet to protect yourself from any fatal accident.

Why should you wear a seatbelt when you drive a car?

You should wear a seatbelt to protect yourself from any kind of accident.

Life is always a narrow escape. You've got to wear the helmet of your own life. You've got to tie the seatbelt of your own life.

Why should you save your money? You should save your money in order to secure yourself in the future if anything happens in your life. You never know who will steal your hard-earned money, and you will die for every single penny. You've got to protect your own life as well as your own money. It is your sole responsibility. There is no guarantee of anything in your life. You can't certify anything in your life.

However, you can save yourself if you take the necessary steps before you execute anything in your life. You can prepare yourself. You can take your own protection before any fatal incident happens. It is, therefore, well quoted that "Prevention is better than cure." You should prevent yourself before anything happens.

Let us suppose that one day when you wake up in the morning, you come to know that that day would be your last day in your life.

What will you do? What will be your reaction? How do you respond?

No doubt, all of a sudden, everything will come to a standstill in your life. You'll lose everything in your life. Your beautiful world will be engulfed by the darkness of despair and sorrow. You have no time to realize anything.

This is just an assumption, but if the same thing were to happen exactly, then what will you do?

If you place yourself in the same scenario, then you'll realize what you have done in your life and what you have missed.

Whatever you want to do in your life, do it right now, because nobody knows what will happen next. You have no time. Anything can happen in your life.

Don't procrastinate anything in your life. Do it right now.

If you have a dream to do something, then do it right now, because you never know what will happen next.

If you have a plan to do something, then do it right now, because you never know what will happen next.

If you have an opportunity to do something, then do it right now, because you never know what will happen next.

You'll regret it in your life if you fail to execute your dreams and plans into your realities. But if you want to enjoy the outcomes of your dreams and plans, then you have to do it right now.

You have to pre-plan for your future because you never know what will happen next. Everything is behind the curtains of your life. You have to act before the curtains of your life unveil.

Don't waste your valuable time. Don't waste your precious life. Make your life meaningful and purposeful. Your life is always in your hands. Only you can protect yourself. Nobody will protect you. You're the savior of your own life.

Anything can happen in your life. Therefore, prepare yourself and work now. Don't procrastinate anything until tomorrow.

⸿***⸿

2. Life is ups and downs

Your life is not always a bed of roses. Sometimes you will find yourself in a bed of roses, and sometimes you will find yourself in a bed of thorns. This is the rule of this world, and you have to accept it.

Life is like a road. You'll never expect the same smooth road all the time. You'll have to drive the car of your life on both smooth and rough roads. You'll have to carry yourself through the ups and downs of your life. If you can navigate the ups and downs of your life successfully, then you'll always make your life smoother in every situation.

The ups and downs of your life are very significant for your growth and development. Without ups and downs, you'll never learn anything, and you'll never gain experience.

Ups and downs are part of your life. There is no person in the entire world who has never faced ups and downs in their life. You'll never walk properly in your life if you never fall down. When you fall down, only then will you learn how to get up.

At every juncture of your life, you'll fall down first; then you'll rise again to make yourself firm and stand tall. But if you rise on your first attempt, it will make it difficult to rise again. It is, therefore, far better to fall first than to rise on the first instance.

Many people rise to great heights in their respective careers on their first endeavors and earn name and fame, along with everything they desire; but when the time of their first fall comes, they can't stand and fall down utterly.

If you see the teeth of a saw, then you'll find that the teeth of a saw are always up and down. Why is it so? If the teeth of a saw are flat, then it will not be able to cut any wood. Therefore, the teeth of a saw are made in the pattern of up and down.

If you observe your own teeth, then you'll see that your teeth are not in the same order; some teeth are up and some teeth are down. Why? This is only to help you bite anything properly with your teeth. Think for a moment: if your teeth were all the same size, then what would happen? You wouldn't be able to bite anything.

If you observe around you, you'll find many more live examples.

Many people are afraid of falling down in their lives, so they never try anything. They remain where they are for their entire lives.

Where there is a fall, there is always a rise. Where there is a failure, there is always success. If somebody loses something, then somebody gains. If somebody weeps, then somebody smiles. This is the law of nature.

Life is a game of rise and fall.

Life is a game of success and failure.

Life is a game of loss and found.

Life is a game of happiness and sorrow.

Have you seen the tides in the sea? The tides of the sea are always rising and falling and create the waves. Why? The tides of the sea are always rising and falling in order to move forward.

In the same manner, if you want to move forward in your life, then you have to learn from your fall in order to rise again. You'll learn more and gain more from your fall than from your rise. You'll learn more and gain more from your failure than from your success.

Always remember that the sun sets every evening in order to rise again the next morning.

Life is always full of ups and downs. Don't be afraid of the ups and downs of your life. Accept them and move on.

‿***‿

3. Everything is not important

Why are many people not happy and content in their lives, even though they have more than enough things to live happily and peacefully? The only reason behind their unhappiness and discontentment is that they always want everything in their lives; they want to do everything in their lives, whether it is important to them or unimportant. They only want to accumulate more things and more stuff, no matter whether it is important to them or unimportant. They fail to differentiate between important things and unimportant things.

What is the most important thing in your life?

The most important thing in your life is to be happy and content with whatever you have. You'll never become happy and content, even if you conquer the entire world.

You must know what is important for you and what is unimportant for you because not everything is important to you. You'll never do everything in your life. You're only capable of doing what you can according to your own potential and caliber.

If a mountaineer takes everything in his climbing bag along with his climbing gear and becomes overweight, then what would happen to him when he climbs? He'll definitely fail to climb the mountain. He has to carry only the important things for his climb, not the unimportant ones.

Suppose you have to travel a long journey; you'll never carry everything with you. You'll only carry those things that are the most important to you throughout your journey.

A doctor can't do the work of a nurse, and a nurse can't do the work of a doctor. A doctor's job is to treat a patient, and a nurse's job is to look after a patient. There is a specialist in every field. There is a certain limitation in every field.

A lion never attacks the herd of animals; he attacks only the weakest and the smallest animals. A lion has a sense that if he attacks the herd of animals, he'll not only hurt himself but also miss his prey.

Think like a lion and work like a lion. Concentrate only on the important one.

Once upon a time, a rich merchant sailed for long-distance trade. He traveled every nook and corner of the world for trading, and he earned a lot of wealth.

Then, after a year, he was returning to his native land. In the middle of his journey, his ship was trapped in a huge sea storm. All his merchant friends and the crew of the ship decided to leave the drowning ship in a small boat, only carrying their important belongings. But the merchant wanted to carry everything along with him in the small boat. Somehow, he managed to load his goods and belongings into the small boat, but the very moment he tried to sail, his boat capsized. The poor merchant drowned, and he lost his life.

When you overload yourself with unwanted things in your life, you'll always drown yourself in the ocean of life.

"A bird in the hand is worth two in the bush." It is a famous proverb. It means it's better to be content with what you have than to risk losing everything by seeking to get more.

If you want to do everything in your life, then you'll always become a loser. You'll never focus on your work. You'll miss the direction of your work. You'll miss everything. But if you do a specific and important thing in your life, then you'll always become a winner and successful.

Now, you've to decide for yourself what you want to become in your life.

A loser or a winner?

What happens when you decide to run everywhere in your life in search of your destiny and goal? Can you reach anywhere? Can you find your destiny? Can you accomplish your goal?

No. Never.

You'll never reach anywhere in your life. You'll never find your destiny in your life. You'll never accomplish your goal. You'll only wander in your life. You'll get nothing; you'll only get disappointments.

If you really want to achieve something great in your life, then just do one important thing with your whole heart, mind, and soul.

If you try to do everything, then you'll fail to do anything in your life.

If you want to reach anywhere, then only do the important things in your life.

If you want to find your destiny, then only do the important things in your life.

If you want to accomplish your goals, then only do the important things in your life.

Only the important things make you an important person in your life.

And the unimportant things make you an unimportant person in your life.

Everything is not important to you. Always focus on the important things in your life.

⁓***⁓

4. Nobody is perfect

Who is perfect in this world? Nobody is perfect in this world. Only Almighty God is perfect in this entire universe.

What is the meaning of perfection?

Perfection means everything is right. Perfection means everything is complete. Perfection means everything is accurate. Perfection means everything is flawless.

Are you right in everything?

No, you're not right in everything.

Are you complete in everything?

No, you're not complete in everything.

Are you accurate in everything?

No, you're not accurate in everything.

Are you flawless in everything?

No, you're not flawless in everything.

Ask yourself. You'll get your answers.

We all want to become perfect in everything. But can we become perfect in everything in our lives?

No.

Can one person become a doctor, an engineer, an architect, a pilot, an actor, a director, a singer, a composer, an artist, an author, and a businessman?

Is it really possible for one person to do all these professions?

No.

We can't become perfect in everything in our lives.

But, yes, we should try to become perfect in our chosen field.

It is always a foolish act if we try to become perfect in everything in our lives.

You'll only become perfect in your chosen field, but not in every field. No doubt, you'll become versatile in some specific field, but not in every field.

Do you know any person who is perfect in every field?

A good coach can't become a good player. And a good player can't become a good coach.

A good director can't become a good actor. And a good actor can't become a good director.

Nobody is perfect in this world. This is the real fact.

Do you find any perfect couples around you?

It is very rare to find a perfect couple. If a husband is tall, then a wife is short. If a husband is thin, then a wife is fat. If a husband is white in complexion, then a wife is dusky in complexion.

You'll never find perfection in everything. Both perfect and imperfect things go hand in hand. You can't deny this fact. You should accept that nobody is perfect in this world.

Think for a moment about what will happen if the fingers of your hands and your legs are all equal in length.

Can you hold anything properly with your hands?

Can you walk properly with your legs?

No. You can neither hold nor walk.

Perfect and imperfect are both our mental states. If you think you're perfect for your work, then the same work is imperfect for another person. If you think the lives of your friends or colleagues are perfect, the same thing is imperfect for them. It is the perspective of our mental states.

Once, a crow was sitting on the branch of a tree. The crow saw two swans swimming in the cool pond. The crow thought, "How happy they are!" When the two swans were flying in the sky, they saw the peacock inside the golden cage in the palace. They thought, "How happy the peacock is inside the golden cage." And when the peacock saw the crow sitting on the branch of a tree, the peacock thought, "How happy the crow is!"

If you think your life is perfect, then your life is perfect. On the other hand, if you think your life is imperfect, then your life is imperfect. And nobody can change your mental status. If you're not perfect in your life, then it doesn't mean that your life will come to an end. It doesn't mean that you'll give up on your life. It doesn't mean that you're incomplete in your life. It doesn't mean that you have no goals and no purpose in your life.

You've to accept your imperfections and try to improve yourself. If you're imperfect in your life, so what? Accept it and move on in your life. It is your golden opportunity to reach your perfection.

Ask yourself why you aren't perfect in your life and what you will have to do to become perfect in your life.

If you do any work in your life, then always give your one hundred percent effort so that if you ever fail to bring perfection to your work, then you wouldn't feel any regret. But at least, you'll reach close to perfection in your work.

If you always try to find perfection in everything, then you'll never find anything. But you'll always become unhappy and discontent in your life. If you always try to find a perfect person in your life, then you'll never find anyone. But you'll always become unhappy and discontent in your life.

A blind man can't give up his life because he can't see with his eyes. But he accepts his imperfection.

A lame man can't give up his life because he can't walk with his legs. But he accepts his imperfection.

A deaf man can't give up his life because he can't hear with his ears.

But he accepts his imperfection.

If you're not perfect, then never give up.

But accept your imperfection.

You have every right to make yourself perfect.

Nobody is perfect in this world. If you're not perfect, then don't worry. Accept your imperfections and try to improve yourself every day.

‿***‿

5. *Never underestimate*

In the epic of Ramayana, the demon king Ravana underestimated that Lord Rama was a human being, an exiled prince of Ayodhya, and hence he abducted Lord Rama's spouse Sita and challenged him. However, Ravana was mistaken. Lord Rama was the incarnation of Lord Vishnu. In the fierce battle between Lord Rama and Ravana, the demon king not only lost his own life but also lost his sons, brothers, relatives, and his entire dynasty.

In the Mahabharata war, the Kauravas underestimated the valor of the Pandavas, and the deadliest war was fought between them. In that war, the Kauravas were decisively defeated by the Pandavas.

Nobody had ever imagined that any country could defeat a superpower like Russia, but a small country from Asia, Japan, had defeated Russia in the Russo-Japanese War (1904-1905) very badly. Russia had underestimated Japanese strength.

The Bollywood industry saw the rise of its first superstar in the 1970s, and Rajesh Khanna's golden era had begun. He delivered many super hit Hindi movies in the 1970s and was the most sought-after hero in the Bollywood industry. However, Rajesh Khanna too had underestimated the young talent at that time, who was struggling in the Bollywood industry. He is none other than today's mega superstar, Amitabh Bachchan. Amitabh Bachchan got an opportunity with his first super hit Hindi movie, Zanjeer. Gradually, the glittering stardom of Rajesh Khanna faded into darkness.

In the world of cricket, nobody could ever imagine that a poor and underperforming team like Bangladesh could ever defeat world champions like India, Australia, South Africa, West Indies, Pakistan, and New Zealand. However, the Bangladesh team has proven that they can defeat any strong team.

In our lives, we, too, many times underestimate the strengths of other people. But we often make mistakes in our assumptions and speculations. In fact, we should never prove anyone to be poor or weak based on our own assumptions and speculations.

You never know who is weaker than you and who is stronger than you. You never know whose preparation is better than yours and whose preparation is lesser than yours.

You should never underestimate the strengths and weaknesses of other people. It will always indicate your weakness if you ever underestimate the strength of others. Therefore, never underestimate anyone in your life; the moment you underestimate the strength of others is the very moment your downfall will begin.

Strong and powerful people never underestimate anyone in their lives. Instead, they always try to improve and develop themselves with their great purposes and noble causes. Instead of underestimating the weaknesses and strengths of others, it is always better to learn from their weaknesses and strengths and enrich your own life.

Never underestimate a small ball of fire,

Because it can burn the entire forest.

Never underestimate a small hole,

Because it can sink the entire ship.

Never underestimate the force of a small bullet,

Because it can kill anybody.

Never underestimate your smallest mistake,

Because it can spoil your entire life.

Never underestimate anybody,

Because you never know who will succeed you and who will defeat you.

Even never underestimate your own potential,

Because you can achieve anything in your life.

Never underestimate anybody. The moment you underestimate the power and strength of other people, that is the very moment your downfall will begin.

༺ *** ༻

6. Solve your own problem

There is nobody in this entire world who has no problems. Everybody has their own problems. You are surrounded by many problems. You can never escape from your own problems. Problems are a part of your life. If one problem arises, then another one will come up. Countless numbers of problems will knock at the door of your life one after another. But if you think that you can bypass your problems, then you are mistaken. You can't. You have to face your problems.

Nobody will solve your problems; only you can solve your own problems. Don't be afraid of your own problems. There is a solution to every problem. Just keep your mind, heart, and soul in proper balance and stability, and at the same time, use your wisdom, knowledge, and experience to counter your problems. You will witness that the problem which seems impossible to solve will become like child's play.

Many people complain that they have family problems, financial problems, health problems, mental problems, and so on. Is there anyone who has no problems at all in their entire lifespan? You will never find anyone.

Family Problems

Many people complain that they have family problems. They have problems with their wives; they have problems with their children; they have problems with their parents; they have problems with their brothers and sisters; they have problems with their relatives, and so on and so forth. If we dig into the real facts, we will discover that they actually have problems with themselves. They can't cope with their own inner conflicts. The real problems that arise in any family or in any relationship are due to a lack of love, respect, and mutual understanding among themselves. Once that lack of love, respect, and mutual understanding is regained, no problem will ever arise in any family or in any relationship.

You can solve your family problems when you restore the lost glory of love, respect, and mutual understanding among your family members.

How to solve your family problems?

→ Love your loved ones unconditionally.

→ Respect your loved ones unconditionally.

→ Respect their feelings.

→ Don't hide anything from them.

→ Be open with them.

→ Treat them as your best buddies.

→ Treat them lovingly and warmly.

→ Understand their needs and requirements.

→ Don't throw your wild card to control them.

→ Lead them by your own good example.

→ Change your own nature.

→ Don't try to change them. You can never change anybody. Only you can change yourself.

Financial Problems

The first and foremost financial problems will only occur when you mismanage your funds in your day-to-day life. When your earnings are less than your expenditures, you will face financial problems.

Mathematically, Earnings < Expenditures

Make your earnings greater than your expenditures.

Mathematically, Earnings > Expenditures

How can you solve your financial problems?

First of all, you must cut down on your extra expenditures; secondly, if possible, increase your income; and thirdly, make a balanced budget for everything in your day-to-day life.

How can you make a balanced budget?

Divide your earnings among all the basic needs of your life, such as daily budget, weekly budget, and yearly budget.

→ For daily needs............Spend 30% of your earnings

→ For domestic purposes...........Spend 30% of your earnings

→ For health-related issues........Spend 10% of your earnings

→ For holidays........................Spend 5% of your earnings

→ For savings..........................Spend 5% of your earnings

→ For investments....................Spend 10% of your earnings

→ For miscellaneous purposes.....Spend 10% of your earnings

Nobody can solve your financial problems. Only you can solve them. Don't wait for anything. If you have financial problems, then solve them as soon as possible. Your financial health is as significant as your own health.

Health Problems

In today's world, everybody has health-related issues. But high blood pressure, diabetes, and sugar are the top three most common health-related issues. Nine out of ten people have these three common health-related issues. Here, I haven't used the term "disease" because these three common ailments are actually not diseases; they are created by us.

How can you overcome your health problems?

The only remedy to cure your health problems is to take care of your body.

→ Take a balanced diet.

→ Eat green leafy vegetables and fruits.

→ Avoid junk food and oily food.

→ Avoid overeating.

→ Avoid alcohol and smoking.

→ Do regular physical exercise.

→ Practice regular meditation and yoga.

→ Treat your body like a temple.

Your health is the biggest wealth in this world. If you lose your health, you will not only lose your money but also lose your mental happiness and peace.

The best solution to solve your problems:

→ Find out the root causes of your problems.

→ Ask yourself: What? Where? When? Why? How?

→ Solve your problems one by one.

→ Don't try to solve your entire problem in one go.

→ View your problems with a positive attitude.

→ Think positively before you solve your problem.

→ Think logically before you solve your problem.

→ Analyze before you solve your problem.

→ Don't be afraid to solve your problem.

→ Don't try to escape from your own problem.

→ Try to convert your problems into new opportunities.

→ Treat your problems like your friends.

→ You're the best person to solve your own problems.

→ Always remember that no problem is greater than you.

Solve your own problem. Nobody can solve your problem. Only you can solve your own problem. Don't try to escape from your own problem. Face your problem and try to find your own solution.

‿***‿

7. Know Yourself

You are the first and the best person to know yourself. If you don't know yourself, then you will never discover your true self. Nobody will come to you to tell you about you. Other people will only tell you about your external looks, such as your face, complexion, body texture, and height. But they can't tell you about your true self.

You have to look deep inside yourself. Once you know how to look within, you will know everything about your true self. And once you know your true self, nobody will stop you from pursuing anything in your life. You will discover the roadmap to your success and glory.

Many people fail to reach their destiny in life because they fail to know themselves. They wander through their lives. Everything is within their reach, but they try to look in the external world. Look into your inner world before you try to look into the outside world, because what is inside you appears in your outside world.

Both the divine person and the devil reside inside you. You have to invoke within yourself what person you want to become in your life. Both greatness and obscurity are hidden inside you. You have to find out who you are. You're the pathfinder of your own life. You're the discoverer of your own life. Whether you're good or bad, only you will know yourself. Whether you're beautiful or ugly, only you will know yourself.

Nobody will feel your happiness, but it's only you who will feel it.

Nobody will feel your excitements, but it's only you who will feel them.

Nobody will feel your anxieties, but it's only you who will feel them.

Nobody will feel your pains, but it's only you who will feel them.

Nobody will feel your wounds, but it's only you who will feel them.

Nobody will know better than you what you like the most.

Nobody will know better than you what you love the most.

Nobody will know better than you what you enjoy the most.

Nobody will know better than you what you taste the most.

Don't follow what other people are doing.

Follow what you like the most.

Don't copy what other people are doing.

Do what you enjoy the most.

Don't imitate how other people are acting.

Act on what you love the most.

If you know you can sing, then sing.

Don't wait for anything.

You know yourself better than anyone.

You're the first person to know yourself.

If you know you can dance, then dance.

Don't wait for anything.

You know yourself better than anyone.

You're the first person to know yourself.

If you know you can act, then act.

Don't wait for anything.

You know yourself better than anyone.

You're the first person to know yourself.

If you know you can play, then play.

Don't wait for anything.

You know yourself better than anyone.

You're the first person to know yourself.

If you know you can work, then work.

Don't wait for anything.

You know yourself better than anyone.

You're the first person to know yourself.

If you know you can write, then write.

Don't wait for anything.

You know yourself better than anyone.

You're the first person to know yourself.

How to know your true self?

Ask yourself the following questions every day:

→ Who am I?

→ What things can I do for myself?

→ In which areas am I good?

→ What are my best hobbies?

→ What are my good habits?

→ What are my strengths?

→ What are my natural talents?

→ What are my best skills?

→ What are the things to which I am naturally inclined?

→ What things do I enjoy the most?

→ What things do I love the most?

→ What things do I like the most?

Write down all the answers in your notebook, think again and again, and meditate on them until you get the right answers.

Finally, you will know your true self.

Nobody knows you better than you do. Only you can know yourself. You're the best person to judge yourself.

⌣***⌣

8. *Accept your errs*

Man is the puppet of errors. We all commit errors in our lives. But we have to accept our errors gladly. Never blame anybody for your own errors. If you commit any mistakes or errors in your life, it doesn't mean that you have committed a grave crime. But accept your errors wholeheartedly, correct them, and move ahead in your life.

Sometimes you blame your parents for your misfortunes. You blame your loved ones for your wrongdoings. You blame your luck and your stars, and sometimes you even blame the situations and time. But in reality, you are just making false excuses to yourself. You're making a fool of yourself.

The best thing to do is to accept your errors, amend them, and move ahead in your life.

One day, a woodcutter bought a new axe from the market. He was very happy and excited to have a new and brand-new axe. The very next day, he went to the forest to cut firewood. He started to cut the best wood for firewood, but he couldn't cut any wood properly. The whole day was wasted. He only managed to cut a handful of firewood. He returned home sadly.

When his wife asked him the reason, he blamed his new axe. His wife asked him, "My dear, did you sharpen your axe before you started cutting the firewood in the forest?"

"No, I didn't," the woodcutter replied.

In our day-to-day life, everybody has a new and brand-new axe, but they all have forgotten to sharpen it before cutting the firewood of their lives. They only start blaming their tools.

What about you?

Blaming is not the solution to your mistakes or errors. Accept your mistakes or errors and figure out your weak points.

If we blame the blowing storm in the rainy season for blowing away our house, then we are just making excuses for our own mistakes, since we haven't mended our house before the rainy season.

You can't always blame the situation and time. You can't change the situation and time in your life, but you can change yourself according to the situation and time. If you know how to change yourself according to the situation and time, then you can do anything in your life; you can achieve anything in your life; nothing is impossible for you. You can manage and adjust yourself in any situation and at any time.

Stop your blame game. Once you cultivate a blame game, you will never do anything in your life. You can't escape from the reality of your life with your blame game. It is an act of foolishness.

You can reach the top of your life when you accept your errors and learn from them. You commit errors in your life only to become the best version of yourself. Never be scared to commit errors in your life. But try to figure out the reasons for your errors. And once you figure out the valid reasons for your errors, you'll know how to amend yourself in your life.

Never blame anybody, but accept your errors. You'll never lose anything if you accept your errors. Amend your errors the very moment you realize.

⌣***⌣

9. Be flexible

Don't make your life too hard and complicated. Don't make your life so busy that you have no time for yourself and your loved ones. Be flexible in your life. If you're too busy and rigid, you'll never enjoy your life fully. Make your life simple and easy. Make your life manageable and controllable.

Everybody has 24 hours in a day. Within these allotted 24 hours, you have to manage your personal life as well as your professional life. You have to do everything in these 24 hours.

If you're flexible in your life, you'll have enough time to enjoy it. You'll never complain about anything in your life. You'll manage your life as well as your family. You'll maintain happiness and peace in your life.

If you're too hard on yourself in your life, then you'll miss the beauty of your life.

If you're flexible in your life, then you'll always enjoy the beauty of your life.

If you're too hard on yourself in your life, then you'll always complain about your life.

If you're flexible in your life, then you'll never complain about your life.

If you're too hard on yourself in your life, then you'll never manage yourself.

If you're flexible in your life, then you'll always manage yourself.

If you're too hard on yourself in your life, then you'll never keep yourself disciplined.

If you're flexible in your life, then you'll always keep yourself disciplined.

If you're too hard on yourself in life, then you'll always experience frustration.

If you're flexible in life, then you'll always find excitement.

If you're too hard on yourself in life, then you'll break down.

If you're flexible in life, then you'll always bounce back after every downfall.

If you're too hard on yourself in life, then you'll fail to handle tough situations.

If you're flexible in life, then you'll always manage yourself in every situation.

If you're too hard on yourself in life, then you'll always hate whatever you do.

If you're flexible in life, then you'll always love whatever you do.

If you're too hard on yourself in your life, then you'll always remain unhappy and disturbed. If you're flexible in your life, then you'll always remain happy and peaceful.

How can you maintain flexibility in your life?

→ Divide your time in such a manner that you'll be able to manage it in your own way.

→ Select what is important to you and what is unimportant.

→ Don't waste your best time on unwanted stuff.

→ Prepare yourself every day.

→ Plan every day.

→ Make a timetable for each day.

→ Don't postpone anything until the next day.

→ Don't try to do too many things at once.

→ Try to keep everything simple and easy.

→ Keep yourself comfortable before you proceed to do anything.

→ Don't be lazy.

→ Be punctual in your personal life as well as your professional life.

→ Just as you never forget to brush your teeth in the morning, never forget to follow your daily responsibilities.

Be flexible in your life. Don't be too tough on yourself. Maintain your own state of mind, body, and soul in proper balance.

⸺***⸺

10. You are not always right

Sometimes we think that we are right, but unfortunately, we are actually wrong. We come to the conclusion too early that we are right and the other people are wrong. Sometimes what we think about a thing, how we see a thing, and even what we believe about a thing, are not as they appear. You may be right, or you may be wrong. Therefore, before you decide what is right and what is wrong, you have to wait for the final outcome. Don't be hasty in giving your verdict.

You're not always right; you may lack knowledge.

Who knows if the other person has more knowledge than you?

You're not always right; you may lack wisdom.

Who knows if the other person has more wisdom than you?

You're not always right; you may lack learning.

Who knows if the other person has more learning than you?

You're not always right; you may lack observation.

Who knows the other person has more observations than you?

You're not always right; you may lack information.

Who knows the other person has more information than you?

You're not always right; you may lack skill.

Who knows the other person has more skill than you?

You're not always right; you may lack experience.

Who knows the other person has more experience than you?

Sometimes parents think that they are right and their children are wrong.

Sometimes children think that they are right and their parents are wrong.

And then problems arise between parents and children.

Sometimes a husband thinks that he is right, and his wife is wrong.

Sometimes a wife thinks that she is right and her husband is wrong.

And then the problems arise between both husband and wife.

In life, what is right and what is wrong depends on time.

In life, what is right and what is wrong depends on the situation.

In life, what is right and what is wrong depends on the place.

In your life, you must remember that the thing which is right for you may not be right for the other person.

You have to respect the feelings of another person.

You have to understand the feelings of another person.

Not all crops are suitable for all seasons. Every crop has its own season to grow; in other words, every crop has its own right time, right situation, and right place to grow and develop.

In the same way, not all things are suitable for you. You have to wait for the right time, right situation, and right place.

You can't fit your right shoes into others' feet.

You can't suit your right outfit on another's body.

You can't impose your right choice on another person.

Everybody has their own likes and dislikes.

You can't force anybody to love what you love.

What is the best solution to find out that you're always right?

In reality, you're always right according to your time, situation, and place. And in the same manner, other people are always right according to their time, situation, and place.

As you respect what is right for you, you also respect what is right for other people.

Don't see with the eyes of egoism.

Try to see both sides of the story.

Don't jump to conclusions too early.

You should never judge anybody based on one viewpoint. You have to wait and watch for other viewpoints.

If you're standing at the right angle, it doesn't mean that the other person is standing at the wrong angle; it may be possible that the other person is standing at the right angle and you're standing at the wrong angle.

In life, you have to complement other people.

If you really want to bring everlasting happiness and peace into your life, then you have to complement your loved ones and everyone else.

You are not always right. Before you give your final conclusion on anything, just wait and try to see the other side of the story.

⸑***⸑

About the author:

Birister Sharma is a full time author. He is also an avid reader. He loves reading, writing, and motivation. He has penned down dozens of self-help motivational books and novels so far.

You may contact him @ birister2007@gmail.com